Samson

The Steller Sea Lion

True Animal Stories, Book 1

Samson the Steller Sea Lion

True Animal Stories, Book 1

By

John Benjamin Sciarra

Acknowledgements

I would like to thank the following people:

Brian Judd: for advice and guidance in distribution and marketing.

Dan Uitti: for his continued guidance even if I don't always take his suggestions.

Pamela Sciarra: my wife and fellow Aquarist whose dedication to animals is unparalleled as well as her compassion and love for the ocean, our God Jehovah, and me (not necessarily in that order).

Aquarists everywhere: I know from personal experience that the vast majority of you take what you do seriously and are dedicated to providing the animals in your care with the greatest love and protection, sometimes, as in my case (not always wisely) to our own peril.

Other Books by Author

- Noah's Diary

- Beachmaster

- Shoestrings — No Time For Dinosaurs, Vol 1

- Shoestrings — Paradox, Vol 2

- Shoestrings — Monster In The Lake, Vol 3

- Shoestrings — Echoes Of Time, Vol 4

- No Time For Dinosaurs — The Novel

- The Most Tragic Love Story Ever Told

- Life at a Public Aquarium, True Animal Stories, Book 2

- And several published short stories, including two award winners.

All available on Amazon Kindle or in paperback.

Author's Foreword

The Steller Sea Lion is currently on the Endangered Species list for one of two populations; Eastern and Western (see Natural History at the end of the story for more info). Both populations had been on the list. However, the Western group is currently considered endangered, while the Eastern population has made somewhat of a recovery, enough to move up to "threatened" status. In the early 1970's, I worked with a member of this species before it was on the list. Steller sea lions kept in captivity, by my estimation, should be limited to rescued animals. These are magnificent creatures, as are many other species of animals, and as such should be afforded the dignity and care that we as humans can provide. Once you read the story of my experiences, I think you will see why I feel this way.

John Benjamin Sciarra

Preface

One day I came into work early and went out to Seal Island as I routinely did to check up on all of the animals. I walked through on the visitor's side first. It was a chilly day with a light rain falling that chilled the bones.

I went into Samson's exhibit after grabbing the pole used to intimidate him by holding it over his head. Samson was a half-ton-plus, Steller sea lion, the largest of the sea lion family, very aggressive by nature and extraordinarily powerful animals. However, Stellers, we learned, will back away from anything that threatens their eyes.

I calmly walked down the tunnel from the service area to the edge of the beach just like I did every other morning. Samson was a couple of feet away and bobbing gently in the water with his eyes closed. He seemed so serene. I lowered the tip of the pole and the next thing I knew, Samson was airborne with a thunderous leap from the water and heading right at me.

The decision was instantaneous. In less time than it takes to blink, I realized Samson had me! I was going to die. I felt that in every bone and fiber in my body. There was no time to raise the pole for protection. Sometimes the rules change. The steadfast rule I always held to was, never back down from an animal. If I hadn't reacted in that very instant, Samson would have flattened me like a bucket of fish.

Adrenalin surged through my bloodstream, and I bolted. I remembered in that split second that a human couldn't outrun a Steller sea lion over rough terrain, but at *that* moment, I was no ordinary person. I was a human who was about to die. I *felt* Samson's breath on my neck as I ran as fast as my short, stubby, Sicilian legs could move expecting the sharp pain that would come as he grabbed me. Everything slowed down like a slow motion movie. I didn't have to think about what my body was doing at that moment. It just reacted.

I couldn't remember if I shut the door behind me. If I had, *I was about to die.*

Introduction

Growing up in a small city like New London Connecticut in the early 1950's, life was much simpler than it is today. I could walk down the middle of Main and Bank Streets and was never in any danger. We had two movie theaters to choose from, and there were always plenty of children's shows. Every movie began with a cartoon with Bugs Bunny or Daffy Duck. Good old Loony Toons! Nowadays, no one walks down that street alone in New London, especially after dark.

My home was fairly typical for the time — family oriented, for the most part. The neighborhood was friendly, and all of us kids hung out together. We played football, basketball, baseball and hide-and-go-seek. Besides loving to climb every tree I could find (and not always with a good outcome), I enjoyed exploring for animals — any animals, much to my mother's annoyance. She was terrified of the snakes, mice, lizards and birds I seemed to find in every corner of the city where there was a patch of woods. Of course, I *had* to adopt them and bring them home. The neighbors could always tell when I brought home a new creature to adopt by my mother's screams.

I suppose I should have known that someday I would devote my life to working with animals. Unlike other children, I didn't want to be a fireman or policeman as essential as those careers might be. I mean, we always had typical pets in my home when growing up, too! I was the oldest of five children, three brothers, and the youngest a sister. Good thing my parents finally had "their little girl" or no telling how many brothers with whom I would have had to fight.

I can't remember the name of the first dog we owned, but I have a rather vivid recollection of an encounter one particular day. I was all gussied up in my Sunday-go-to-meeting clothes and decided to go outside in our backyard to play with our over stimulated mongrel.

I don't remember the details of the encounter except to say that I looked like I had been ravaged by wolves when my grandfather came to my rescue. Fortunately, the damage was all superficial with my clothing receiving the majority of the damage as the dog had ripped holes in my pants and jacket. I'm not sure of the animal's eventual outcome except he was no longer a

Could have been my first dog!

member of our family. And I didn't have to go to church that day, either!

We soon got another pet; a female collie mix my father named Lassie. The television show starring a male dog with a female name (the indignity of it all!), was quite popular in the 1950's when I was in my youth.

***

My father took up an unusual hobby: aquarium keeping! We had a small aquarium with several common goldfish, as I recall. Not many people had an aquarium back then as a hobby, as the aquarium industry was entering its infancy. My father was always a little ahead of everyone else.

Aquarium keeping is a great hobby and can teach children responsibility. Just don't pet the fish!

We were the first to have a television on our block because my dad went to school for television repair and worked for a company called Modern Electric in New London. Of course, it was black and white and not much bigger than today's computer tablets. We were one of the first to have a color set when they became available as well. Imagine having to walk all the way across the living room just to change to one of three channels!

Well...Dad was *proud* of his fish and liked to show them off to all the relatives and the many friends he had through his work. However, the fish always died after a time. My father was puzzled as to the cause — that is until one day he came home from work and found his number one son petting the goldfish.

"Johnny! What are you doing with the fish?"

"I'm just petting them, Daddy."

"Petting them! You can't pet fish!"

"But, why, Daddy? I pet Lassie, and she likes it!"

I don't think the sparkling eyes and charming wit worked. I was forbidden to touch the fish. In later years, however, I ignored that rule and stroked all manner of marine life from moray eels to whales and everything in between. Of course, by then I knew the rules.

Or did I?

Chapter One

SAMSON

Ad in classifieds: "Free to good home. Two-year-old Steller Sea Lion. Cute. Needs room to run and a BIG pool. Weighs over a half ton. Mate included."

No, this ad didn't really appear in any newspaper, but it should have!

This story is all about working with marine animals at a public aquarium. The star of the book is a Steller sea lion by the name of Samson. Samson weighed in at over 1000 pounds! That's a half-ton of animal literally and figuratively. He was twelve feet long and had four, six-inch long interlocking canines. His jaws could exert a pressure around 2000 pounds per square inch! He was exceedingly aggressive by nature. It was a survival instinct designed to drive only the strongest male to breed with the sea lion colony. It was this attitude that made training Samson the most frightening experience of my life. I still occasionally have nightmares some 30 years later.

The Steller sea lions' natural home or habitat is off the coast of Alaska and Northern California. They reside on a group of islands called the Aleutian Islands in the Bering Sea and specifically the Pribilof Islands. The beaches there are inhabited by, not only the Steller sea lion but also the Northern Elephant Seal and the Northern Fur Seal.

Can you imagine what it must be like to be "THE BEACHMASTER" on one of those islands? Being the Beachmaster is little like playing "King of the Hill." Only the biggest and strongest male called a bull, can rule the beach and mate with all of the females. The group of females is called a harem. All of the other males wanted to defeat the Beachmaster and frequently challenged him to a fight. It is that kind of environment that Samson would have grown up in had he not been placed in captivity. There is no doubt in my mind; Samson would have been the beachmaster!

A bull Steller sea lion

The staff at the Mystic Marinelife Aquarium (now called the Mystic Aquarium) in Connecticut where I worked

8

first heard about Samson when we received word of his imminent arrival. What we didn't know is that *everyone in the world* had heard of Samson. Everyone, that is, except us. And no one else wanted him because they were too afraid to handle Samson! Just how dangerous an animal Samson would become, we wouldn't find out for some time.

***

Since Steller sea lions are aggressive, powerful, agile and dangerous in their natural habitat, no one could really expect that they would be any more docile in captivity. If you're afraid of big dogs like Rottweilers, Dobermans or pit bulls, this definitely isn't the animal for you. We had just built a state-of-the-art exhibit for seals and sea lions called "Seal Island." Samson was going to be our star attraction.

Northern Fur Seal

The Pribilof exhibit was originally designed to house a collection of pugnacious fur seals. The Aquarium's plans had to be changed, however, when the permit to collect them was tied up in red tape. However, we couldn't open Seal Island without *something* in the exhibit! That something, it was decided, would be the most spectacular animal I had ever seen—but not at first sight.

***

The day Samson arrived was a warm one. There wasn't a cloud in the sky, and the staff at the Aquarium was excited. A large holding tank in a wire enclosure was built to house Samson and his mate. Her name was, no—not Delilah—but Josie. That didn't seem right, so the first thing we did was change her name. We promptly renamed her Delilah. She didn't seem to mind. Delilah was small in comparison to her partner. A mere slip of a sea lion at 700 pounds, Delilah was a beautiful, sleek animal with smooth silver, gray hair. She was never aggressive and easily trained. Samson also appeared easy to train, but not before he tested me to the maximum. Samson arrived in an enormous crate that looks like it was designed to hold the *Velociraptors* from "Jurassic Park." I think Samson would have scared the daylights out of the dinosaurs. As we opened the door to the truck that had transported him from the airport, I could hear low gurgling noise coming from the back of the cab. He didn't *sound* dangerous.

Cautiously, we began to move the cage out of the truck with a *come-along*, a pulley device used to move heavy objects. When we had the cage far enough out of the back of the truck, I jumped up on top and opened the large sliding door. Instead of the ferocious monster I had been expecting, there on the floor of the cage was a weary-eyed, pathetic looking sea lion that looked more like a B-52 jet bomber that had crash landed instead of the mythical dragon whose reputation was known throughout the entire world (excluding us, of course). Apparently, Samson had motion sickness.

Once we had coaxed Samson out of his traveling cage and into his new pool (which took the better part of the day), he started to perk up a bit. The ice cold spring water welling up from deep under the Aquarium grounds must have felt refreshing to him. He and Delilah began swimming around in the cold water. It was small—too small to hold the two of them, but this was to be a *very* temporary holding facility. Seal Island was due to be completed within a few weeks of their arrival, so they weren't going to be there very long.

I had begun the habit of going into the exhibit and sitting at the edge of the redwood deck where the animals could haul out and sun themselves. I even felt comfortable enough to dangle my bare feet in the water. Samson began eating pretty well and showing signs of coming to life— perhaps too much. One day after a couple of weeks I entered the enclosure and had the daylights scared out of me. Samson flew out of the water right at me! There were only a couple of feet before the entrance gate, and I dove through a split second before Samson slammed into it. From that point onward, I decided the best course of action was to feed Samson *through* the fence until we moved him to his new exhibit. I wondered; *what was it going to be like once we moved Samson into the Pribilof Island exhibit?* The reality proved to be far worse than my worst nightmares.

Chapter Two

MOVING DAY

The day finally came when we were ready to move Samson and Delilah to Seal Island. It was a bright, beautiful spring day and everyone at the Aquarium was excited. Early in the morning, we drained the small pool leaving Samson and Delilah in the bottom. They knew something was going on and watched us with wide-eyed curiosity.

A small crane arrived, and it was just tall enough to reach over the eighteen-foot-high fencing surrounding the pool. Samson became agitated when the top of the crane appeared over the enclosure—with me on top of the crate! Once we had the crate positioned on the bottom, Samson tried to join me on top of the crate. I didn't think that was such a good idea and managed to discourage him with my foot, kicking at him just to let him know I didn't appreciate the company.

I lifted the door to one side of the crate and waited to see if he would go in. He looked into the crate and then at me. Then he sat with his head off to one side and closed his eyes. It was almost as if he were intentionally ignoring me. Maybe Samson remembered the recent experience in transit and the sickness he felt. I don't know. Sometimes it's just impossible to tell what an animal is thinking. I tried throwing fish in the crate. He just looked at the fish—

longingly. It wasn't enough, though. No amount of coaxing seemed to work.

I decided to try another idea. I opened the gate to the *other* side. Now, Delilah got into the act and began looking into the crate. Samson kept pushing her out of the way. Perhaps his competitive nature was getting the better of him, but he decided to venture in and grab the fish before Delilah. Samson inched his way in, and I sat poised ready to drop the gate at a second's notice. Samson backed out again and snorted and growled at me. He was becoming agitated with this giant box in the middle of his pool and now began circling as if he were trying to figure out how to get the fish without actually going into the crate.

Female Steller

Suddenly, he charged into the cage and grabbed the fish. I wasn't about to miss this opportunity. I dropped the gate behind him feeling he was going to try and back out first. My instincts were correct. As he backed into the gate, I dropped the one in front before he had time to react. I had him! Now Samson was *really* agitated. He was growling and snarling and baring his teeth like an angry dog. I was concerned that, now I was really on his bad side.

I stepped off the crate and went out the door to the enclosure as the crane operator lifted Samson out. We secured a couple of lines to the crate to keep it from swinging. It was a good thing, too, because he was racing back and forth inside the cage. I wondered if he was worried about another plane ride. Quickly the crane operator lowered the crate, and we began the slow trip to Seal Island holding the crate and trying to keep it from swinging. Samson calmed down, but he didn't seem too happy with the situation.

***

There was a second *much* larger crane awaiting us at Seal Island. It was enormous with an extension near ninety feet. To me, it looked more like the *Leaning Tower of Pisa*! It was necessary to have the added length to be able to reach the middle of the Pribilof Islands exhibit. I hopped back up on top of the crate figuring the operator would lift us up and over the three-foot high wall. No big deal. I wasn't the least bit worried. I held onto the guide wires as the winch began to lift the crate rather suddenly.

It became apparent to me that more height was needed as I reached the 30-foot mark — but the operator kept lifting. At first, I thought the lever had jammed. Looking up and seeing the pulley at the top of the crane coming towards me, I grabbed the guide wire with both hands. My knuckles were turning white. My face probably was a little pale about right then, too. I was glad the photographer from *The New London Day* newspaper didn't have a telephoto lens because it would have shown the look of terror on my face.

Once back on solid ground without any mishap (I thought the lines were going to break and Samson, and I were going to plummet to the earth with tremendous force, and my life was going to end), I regained my composure and released Samson to explore his new home. We went back and got Delilah. However, this time I declined the ride over and waited until the cage was in the middle of the exhibit before jumping over and releasing her. We filled the exhibit with water, and Samson appeared excited and splashed about playfully with Delilah. Little did I know what was in store for me in the near future with this animal.

Chapter Three

SAMSON LEARNS SOME NEW "TRICKS"

Once we began training Samson, he learned at a phenomenal rate. Initially, only the Head Trainer, Harry and I were allowed to even go near Samson and Delilah. These new challenges to Samson's intellect (some might object to my use of this word, but I can think of no better way to describe him) appeared to stimulate him. He learned to "hold" in about five minutes. He quickly understood that he had to keep his nose in contact with the ball *until* I gave him the *bridge* that signaled the behavior complete. I decided to eliminate the whistle all together and used only the vocal command, "Good!" Having a whistle in my mouth was too much of a distraction. Whenever I was around Samson, I needed my wits about me. There were still too many unknowns about this animal.

It wasn't but a couple of sessions with both Harry and I working him that we were able to wean him off the ball and have him—ever-so-carefully—hold on our closed fist. By having him extend his neck all the way forward, we knew he couldn't physically bite us. He would have had to recoil his head much like a snake can't strike without recoiling first. At least that's what we surmised, and it turned out to be the case. However, in one instance he did snap at one of the handlers we brought in later on. If he didn't know *you* as an individual, he would make you earn his respect.

Harry and I had established a relationship with Samson. Anyone else we brought into the exhibit Samson challenged. Samson wasn't mean or cruel. That was just the way it is in his world. After all, Samson would have eventually become the beachmaster if he had been back in the rookery in the Pribilofs.

In a few cases, I would introduce a new trainer by bringing them into the exhibit with me. I'd tell them beforehand that Samson would charge them. I emphasized that they couldn't run or back down in any way. One day a new trainer did flinch, and Samson by-passed the seat and went straight for him. He responded by turning and running for it. Wrong. *Very wrong*. Samson would have caught him and torn him to shreds if I hadn't jumped in front of the charge and screamed, "NO!" Samson stopped cold and growled at me, but he backed down. He still viewed me as the beachmaster of this beach. It wouldn't always be that way. We didn't know it at the time, but we were playing a dangerous game. In retrospect, we were fools. Ask me to do it again, and I'd join the circus and swing from a high wire before I'd face an animal like Samson on his terms. My control over him was always—*always* weak at best.

Chapter Four

CLOSE CALL

Four, six-inch, interlocking canines with a jaw pressure of two-thousand pounds per square

A cardinal rule when working with aggressive

animals is: *never run from an animal.* While there are exceptions (you'll see later what I mean), the result of running away only increases the chance of catastrophe. What may have started out as posturing by the animal might quickly — instantaneously — turn into a predator-prey response. In case you're wondering, *you* become the prey when you turn and run. So, unless you're the world's fastest sprinter?

To illustrate this, I offer the following experience.

One day, after we had moved Samson and Delilah into the California Coast exhibit, one of our aquarists (what we call animal caretakers in the professional aquarium business) went out to feed the California sea lions, of which there were around 20, and three young elephant seals. At that time we were feeding Samson away from the beach as he was disrupting the other sea lions. Bob entered the exhibit under a cliff. I had stressed to Bob the importance of not flinching should Samson threaten him, even from the water.

"Unless you want to invite Samson to join you, *hold your ground at all costs.* It could mean your life," I told him.

Melodramatic? Hardly. Samson continuously tested all of us randomly with subtle head moves and quick charges to see how we would react. An aquarist had to be on his or her toes *constantly.* Back in the Pribilof Islands exhibit, I could stand within inches of Samson, which I did to prove this point both to myself and the rest of the staff. He would throw his head at my leg — within inches. I staunchly held my ground. Samson might perceive even a slight movement as a retreat and have been on top of me faster than I could blink. Of course, I always gave my supervisor a near heart attack with these tactics. What I was doing was defining *my territory.* Even subtle changes like cracks and depressions in the beach could denote a territorial boundary. To step over that line was a challenge to fight.

I outlined my territory by carefully examining the topography of the beach. Then I selected the areas I would "defend." It was a dangerous game, and I almost lost more than my territory sometime later.

On this particular day, I just happened to walk by the exhibit as Bob emerged from under the cliff to feed Samson. I was on the visitor's side, and there was no one there at the moment. Samson caught sight of Bob and charged at him from the water leaving a wake behind him. Bob was completely caught off guard and *backed away* from the edge of the beach. That's all that Samson needed. He was out of the water in a flash and about to pin Bob against the back wall. Petrified, Bob froze.

Bob's life was in *imminent danger.* Without thinking, I did the stupidest thing I ever did. I leaped over the railing and hung just above the pool screaming Samson's name. Samson turned away from Bob and decided that I was a more appealing target! He dove back into the pool and headed with a speed run under water and leaped. The instant he cleared the water, I was up and back over the railing and screaming at Bob, who was still frozen in fear, to get out. I *shudder* when I think back on this incident. *What if I had lost my grip?* If I had fallen into the water, I was as good as dead. Fortunately, I didn't.

I had to scream at Bob several times to get him to move. He came to his senses a moment before Samson remembered what he had been doing, and ran out leaving a bucket of flattened fish on the beach. It was a close call — too close. But it wasn't the last time. Bob seemed to have a penchant for getting himself in trouble.

Again, as chance would have it, I happened to be walking by the California Coast exhibit. I didn't see Samson anywhere, which I thought, was odd. Bob should have been out feeding him. I thought, perhaps Samson was up in the tunnel near the sliding door waiting. Bob would have to exercise caution if that were the case. Then I heard, "Oh crap!" That didn't sound right, so I ran around past the Pribilof exhibit and into the back area. What I saw stopped me cold in my tracks.

Samson was walking around by the small holding pool *inside the backup area.* Bob had assumed his usual position of being frozen in fear up against a sliding door leading to another exhibit. Fortunately for him, Samson became engrossed in his new surroundings. Samson, with Delilah in tow, was now looking in my direction. I closed a metal gate that led to the food prep area behind me. Samson cautiously approached me, and I yelled to Bob to get out through the New England coast exhibit behind him and to shut the door tight. He managed to do this. Now there was another problem. How was I going to get Samson and Delilah back into the exhibit?

Samson blocked the gate and wouldn't respond to my commands. I decided to try and get on the other side of him by climbing up and over the top of the gate. There was enough room to squeeze through. Then it was a simple matter of getting over the top of the fencing surrounding the holding pool. It was empty at the moment. Samson kept trying to get at me, but I moved too fast for him. He was growling at me now. I think he wanted to claim the room as his territory. That was not going to happen!

Standing safely behind the fencing, I felt much braver. I taunted Samson. He came over and sniffed at my foot, which was up against the fence. Then I surprised him by kicking the chain-link fencing catching him lightly in the nose. It startled him. I yelled as loudly as I could. Samson, not comfortable in the enclosed environment, retreated into the exhibit. Delilah quickly followed.

I ran out and shut the door. After that incident, I decided that Bob would be better off working with the smaller animals before we had a dead aquarist on our hands. I don't think he minded.

***

It was clear to me I had to come up with a way of training Samson to stop his attacks. Harry, the Head Trainer, had much more experience as a trainer than I and he suggested *I train him to attack me.*

"No, you don't understand. I want him to *stop* attacking me! Are you insane?"

He countered with this illustration.

"Let's say you have a dog that digs holes in your backyard and you want him to stop."

"Cut off his legs?" (I was just kidding, but I couldn't resist).

"Seriously. Every time he digs a hole, you reward him."

"Seems to me that will make him dig more holes."

"Yes, it will."

"Okay, now I'm confused…"

"Have you ever heard of a behavioral process known as *extinction*?"

"Yes," I lied. I didn't want to seem stupid. After all, here he is teaching me to have my dog dig up my yard.

"Here's how it works. You give him a signal to dig. He responds by digging. You can even blow a whistle. Once he responds to this with some consistency, you simply stop rewarding him. Eventually, he'll stop digging holes. Get it?"

"Sure. Just one question though."

"Yeah?"

"Is this before or after he digs the swimming pool?"

How much further to China?

Actually, the principle really was ingenious!

When Samson charged at me, I blew a whistle and rewarded him with a fish. Then I trained him to charge me with a hand signal. I gave the signal, and he charged across the water at me. Just before he reached me, I blew the whistle, said, "Good, boy!" and pointed for him to go back to his seat.

Once I had him doing this consistently, I stopped giving him his reward: the fish. After giving him the command to attack and then not rewarding him, he finally got fed up with the whole thing and ignored my commands. *Extinction!*

What I had done was to change the *motive* for the attack. Instead of attacking me to challenge me, I had changed the natural behavior into a controlled one. It's called *behavior modification*. Samson stopped charging people — until breeding season. Then *all the rules changed.*

Chapter Five

AGGRESSION!!!

As I indicated earlier, the male Steller sea lion is particularly aggressive by nature. The drive to be the Beachmaster is intense. As young Samson reached puberty, things began to change. He started picking on the other animals—and the elephant seals, not being particularly quick, soon became his favorite target.

Samson was relentless in chasing all three of the young seals. The California sea lions were usually too fast for Samson (except for a couple of exceptions I'll relate shortly). So, to vent his aggressive tendencies, Samson chased the elephant seals and, unknown to us, frequently bit them with his six-inch long canines.

We first became aware of the problem when I noticed a swollen area on Gurgle's side. Upon closer examination, I realized it was severely abscessed—a vast area filled with fluid from infection. I called the veterinarian immediately and placed Gurgle in a squeeze cage, a device made of thick steel bars to immobilize the larger animals for extensive examinations and drawing blood.

Our veterinarian found several more areas with abscesses. He cut these open to allow for drainage. It fell to the aquarists, and more specifically me, to continually open the area with a long Q-tip-like cotton probe and break up the area of tissue to allow the abscess to drain. The danger was that it might become *systemic*, that is, an infection that attacks the whole body. If that happened, it could quickly become life threatening.

The hardest part of this for all of us was the screams of the elephant seals as we dug into the damaged area. Our veterinarian was reluctant to use any anesthetic to kill the pain because of the unique physiology of the seals — particularly, the animals' ability to hold its breath so long and dive incredibly deep.

Young Northern Elephant Seal

What allowed them to do this is the unusual ability of the muscles to retain oxygen and squeeze blood out of its extremities. Without going into a biology lesson here, suffice it to say that the anesthetics of the time could easily have caused the seals to go into this deep dive reflex and never wake up. There were many reports in the field from other marine mammals of this happening, and we didn't want to lose our precious elephant seals!

While it was extremely difficult for me to hurt the animals in this way, I blocked out the screams as best I could and tried hard to remember that, if I didn't clean the abscessed areas out thoroughly every day, they could die. The other aquarists didn't want the responsibility, and the veterinarian lived an hour away.

One day, Gurgle got me back. I was moving the elephant seals with a large plywood board. Sometimes we did this to protect ourselves among groups of seals and sea lions. Our veterinarian was examining another animal, and I had Gurgle corralled. He was calm and relaxed. He also became a little curious.

Gurgle stuck his neck out and around the board and spotted my leather boot. It probably smelled of fish and seal feces. He rubbed his sensitive vibrissae back and forth over my boot. I didn't notice.

Apparently, he wasn't satisfied with this examination of my boot. He reached out and opened his mouth to taste it. He grabbed the back of my boot and gave it a squeeze. I now knew what kind of pressure these animals could exert. While there was little danger of him biting through the boot, the mere pressure put on the heel of my foot almost caused me to pass out from the pain. I felt he could have crushed my foot right through the thick boot! I was much more careful after that.

Full grown male Northern Elephant Seal

Chapter Six

THE PLAN

"We need a good plan — Ya THINK!"

T his was the day we first decided to train the untrainable: Samson. And this part of the story goes back to the time when we first introduced Samson and Delilah into their new home at the Pribilof Island exhibit. Harry and I decided we were going to be the first people in the United States to train a Steller sea lion — and live to tell about it.

Our plan was relatively simple — on paper anyway. Our only previous incursion onto the beach resulted in

Samson flying out of the water and charging across the beach in our direction. We made the decision not to stay around at that time to see what his intentions were but reasoned it wasn't for a hug. I could vividly see the headlines in the newspaper the following day: "Mac Truck-like Animal Flattens Trainers in Mystic." It was then we decided we needed a *plan!*

Drawing on the facts we had accumulated and our combined experience training animals, we decided that the best approach would be to go into the exhibit and establish *our* territory. We reminded ourselves that, although Samson seemed pretty smart for an animal, he was still just an animal. *We* had superior intelligence. *We* would convince Samson that we were just as big, if not—that *we* were *The Beachmasters!* [Incidentally, I wrote a novel called "Beachmaster" based on a Steller sea lion escaping a public aquarium and wreaking havoc in several New England towns!]

The logical part of our minds told us this would work. Our hearts, on the other hand, required considerable convincing—even for a couple of guys with a bit of a death wish. I'll spare you the reasoning behind that except to say we were both going through some traumatic experiences in our lives.

Now, we both reasoned that a blow to the neck would convince Samson he had been injured and that he would, hopefully, back down in a confrontation for the rookery; in this case, the Pribilof Island exhibit. The question became: "How could we safely deliver such a blow?" It was a very dangerous idea since, if it didn't work, we could at the very least be critically injured; we might even die.

We finally decided after looking at our options that we could use a wooden oak handle from a garden shovel. It was about three feet long, which meant we were going to have to get pretty close. We both would carry one as well as a whistle and a bucket of fish. Our plan was to walk boldly out onto the beach while Samson was swimming in the pool. We picked our battlefield — an area about midway across the beach. If we were wrong about any of this, there would be no chance of escape. Steller sea lions can outrun a human over rough terrain — or so we had read. I was hoping we wouldn't have to test that premise. However, we could see no other way to manage this animal in captivity. It was the biggest challenge we would ever face in our lives!

***

THE PLAN consisted of the following:

1. Holding our ground while Samson charged. To turn and run at this point, we felt, meant certain death. So, we had to be committed (perhaps we should have been *committed*).

2. Once Samson came to a halt (which we were counting on) and lunged at us, we would step forward and deliver a blow to his chest and yell loudly, "NO!" Samson had about six inches of blubber in this area of his body, so we knew it wouldn't injure him in any way, but it would make a loud thud.

If he had been on a rookery and fighting the beachmaster for possession of the harem, the beachmaster would have sunk his teeth in with the blow. It's still unlikely Samson would have felt pain. We surmised instinct would have kicked in and Samson would have backed down.

3. We would then step forward and deliver a second blow and yell, "POOl!" Then we would gesture towards the water. We realized this was stretching his level of comprehension. At this point, logic began to dissipate. Would Samson have the intelligence to connect this gesture?

Usually, with California sea lions, it takes some time for them to respond to a gesture—in reality, it held little meaning to the sea lion. The trainer could have picked his nose (sorry—my hyperboles can get a little extreme) and the animal would do whatever he had been trained to respond to as a hand signal purely by association with the behavior followed by the reward (the fish in the case of a sea lion). Our lives depended on Samson being able to follow this gesture—*literally*.

4. Once Samson went into the water we would blow a whistle and *immediately* throw him a fish.

5. If Samson approached the beach again, we would say, "NO!" If he continued, we would have to step forward again and deliver another blow. It wasn't cruel or harmful. Our intent was NEVER to hurt Samson in any way.

In all my years of working with animals, the only difference I saw between those who became animal activists or those who became animal handlers was the way they responded to the *management* of the animals. Both parties felt pain in their hearts when animals' lives were on the line. The animal handler, however, must take responsibility to act in the animals' best interest.

I'm probably not going to make any friends saying this, and my intention is not to hurt anyone, but animal activists are like back-seat drivers. They want *you* to "fix it" without taking any responsibility themselves. Some extremists will try and injure humans whose lives they place below that of the animal and that, quite simply, is morally wrong any way you try and justify it.

For example, locally in Groton, Connecticut where I live there has been an issue over deer hunting in a place called Bluff Point. To control the deer population, the state has allowed hunting on the Bluff at very specific times during the year. It is very controlled. The animal rights activists have vehemently objected to this so-called slaughter of "Bambi."

But consider the consequences of not acting to control the population. First, there is the increase in auto accidents when the deer venture off the Bluff to forage in people's yards for food. The deer usually loses and, occasionally, so does the driver of the vehicle. If you've ever seen one of these accidents, it leaves an impression. It is not a pretty sight, and I've seen several.

Secondly, if the deer population isn't *culled*, it results in disease and even starvation. To my way of thinking, it is by far crueler to stand idly by while *any* animal starves to death. Hungry animals are much more susceptible to disease, which can then spread through the herd quickly. Would some argue that this is a more humane way to manage the deer population than allowing a hunt whereby the meat is eaten and even donated to feed a hungry person, which is often the case? I guess that's a personal decision everyone has to make. Incidentally, I don't eat meat of any kind primarily for health reasons.

In the case of training animals in captivity, we become directly responsible for managing all aspects of the animals' care. Sometimes it means acting contrary to our heart's inclinations.

So too, a parent disciplines a child. Not by hurting the child, but by training him or her. A baby touching an electrical cord may need a tap on the wrist to indicate that this is dangerous. By *no means hard to enough to hurt the child*, but as an insult, so to speak. A child will realize he has displeased his parent and wants to correct that by, shall we say at this point, instinct in much the same way an animal might respond? Not so much to please the handler. After all, the handler *is* the source of food for the captive animal. The objective should *always – always,* be to the benefit of the animal as an individual when possible or the entire herd when necessary.

I might also add that the preferable method is to employ *positive* reinforcement. That would have to come later if we lived through this encounter! I wonder what our epitaph would have read. Oh, never mind.

Let me move on to the rest of The Plan:

6. Assuming we were still alive (we both approved of this part of the plan), we would then reposition ourselves next to the entrance that led through a tunnel some twenty feet in length, and a large sliding metal door.

A large boulder was situated right at the bottom of the entrance tunnel next to a shallow area designed for young pups to swim. It was a fiberglass catwalk built just below the surface of the water and covered with small rocks, and it was durable enough to hold Samson's weight. We decided this would be the best place in the exhibit to feed and train him (see how optimistic we could be?).

Once we had him in the water, we would slap the rock and say, "Seat!" Samson would be allowed to approach the rock *only* from the shallow pool. This way we had a barrier and time to react should Samson catch us off guard with another charge. This decision, it turned out, saved more than one life in the treacherous business of working with Samson.

***

We submitted our plan in exceptional detail to my supervisor. He looked at us like we had just stepped off another planet.

"Are you guys both out of your minds? This is insane! There's no way I can let you do this!"

"But Jeff," I said. "How else are we going to take care of the exhibit? We're all going to look pretty stupid throwing fish over the wall. Some public aquarium we are!"

Jeff retorted, "You're going to get killed if you do this! I won't have that on my conscience."

"It's a risk we're willing to take, Jeff. It's our lives." I looked to Harry for support.

"John's right, Jeff. There's just no other way. We'll have to put Samson down if we can't care for him."

Jeff wouldn't budge. I had no recourse but to acquiesce. After all, Jeff was *my* boss. On the other hand, Harry didn't work for Jeff. He was the Curator of the Marine Theater and reported directly to our Vice President. Our VP reviewed the plan carefully and, despite Jeff's pleading, the plan was approved. We were *both* to report directly to the VP as far as training Samson was concerned. Jeff was off the hook if we died. It would have rested on the VP's shoulders, and he felt we weren't going to fail. We both found this encouraging, and we needed all the encouragement we could get!

Chapter Seven

PUTTING THE PLAN INTO ACTION

Just who is training whom?

The night before we were to initiate our plan, I barely slept. I kept picturing in my mind how it would go. Harry and I decided that to whomever of us Samson directed his charge would take the initiative. The other would step back to avoid confusion.

Harry and I agreed to meet early over coffee and psyche each other up. We *had* to know positively that this approach would work. If either of us panicked and ran—we were as good as dead. We sincerely believed that.

We asked for an observer on the public side of the exhibit to call the hospital in case of an emergency, although I'm sure a coroner would have been more appropriate. We wanted to get this all over with long before the crowds began to arrive. We didn't even tell Jeff. His presence would have been a distraction for us. There could be absolutely no negative influence present, or we might have changed our minds.

We went to the front of the exhibit and ascertained that Samson was swimming quietly in stereotypical fashion (the kind of behavior lions exhibit in zoos walking in a pattern over and over. It meant that Samson needed stimulation) in the pool. Then we went inside.

The door to the exhibit was eight feet by six feet and quite heavy. It slid to the right on casters along the top and bottom. We kept it bolted from the inside and under lock and key. It wouldn't have been good to have some night security get curious and inadvertently walk in on Sammy. It was a straight shot up the tunnel from a narrow corridor at the base of the tunnel just to the left of the boulder we intended to use for Samson's seat. We hoped he wouldn't figure that out.

Gently we slid the door aside being careful not to make a sound. We wanted to be in position before Samson was aware of our presence. Each of us had a bucket of fish, a whistle and our version of a rolled up newspaper: our three-foot long oak handles. The clubs seemed wholly inadequate, and the first fringes of nervousness appeared. *What were we doing?* Nothing short of a rocket launcher was going to stop him if he decided to come after us. Psychology would have to prevail.

Quietly we walked down the tunnel. It seemed much longer than usual today. I almost wondered if there was going to be a light at the end of the tunnel. We left the door open about half way — just in case we needed to get away and beat him to the entrance. Harry went to the right — I went left. I had a sinking feeling and struggled with the urge to back out. I later learned Harry felt the same way. There was no backing out now.

***

I called out once in position, "Samson!"

He was at the farthest end of the pool when he abruptly stopped swimming and poked his head up out of the water. At first, he didn't spot us. Then he snorted when he did and swam quickly toward the beach leaving a white wake behind him like a speedboat racing across a lake. In one motion he leaped out of the water, onto the beach and, growling ferociously, he charged — straight at *me!*

I was terrified! It was as if I were standing in the middle of the train tracks while waiting for the train to hit me. My knees began to wobble, and my legs started to buckle. I could feel the veins in my neck and back tighten starving off the oxygen to my brain. I remember the discussion my conscious mind was having with my unconscious mind, which was desperately trying to take over. Passing out was the wrong thing to do here! My body seemed to be determined to make that happen. If I passed out now, it was all over. I struggled to keep my composure — *barely*.

Samson charged to within about three feet of me. I wasn't sure he was going to stop, but I couldn't let him see me flinch. The look in his eyes was frightening — demonic comes to mind. I read that someone described their eyes that way: *demonic*. It fit. They were a murderous-looking dark brown — almost black — surrounded by a thin line of white conjunctiva. His nostrils flared, and his four, six-inch interlocking canines were clearly visible. The Stellers' jaws have the ability to exert over several thousand pounds of pressure per square inch — enough to do some serious damage!

Samson lunged with tremendous force straight at my chest stopping only an inch away — *literally*. At the same time, he roared a deep, penetrating, bone-shattering sound. I was sure there was now a hole clean through my back.

It should have paralyzed me. The *infrasound* of animals, such as lions and tigers, has that effect on prey. They emit a sound so deep and bass and so low, that you could feel it. The human ear can't hear the low-frequency sound waves of infrasound. It is designed to freeze the prey long enough to strike. I was currently the recipient of such a tactic at that moment.

The effect it had on me surprised even me. I became *angry* but remembered what I had been rehearsing for days (and nights). As Samson recoiled, no doubt to strike again, I stepped *toward* him and hit him in the chest with the oak handle. At the same time, I think I implemented my own brand of infrasound, however, higher it may have been at that moment. I yelled as loudly and deeply as possible, *"NO!"*

Samson stepped back with a look on his face I can only describe as complete astonishment. It was if he were saying to himself, "I can't believe this *puny* little human has just struck me! *No* one has *ever* dared challenge *me*. I am the *King of the Beach*!"

Before he could consider his options, I stepped forward and struck him in the chest again. "Pool!" I yelled and then gestured emphatically by pointing toward the water. Samson backed away from me a step. He looked confused.

Again I stepped forward and struck him and said, "Pool!" I repeated the gesture of pointing toward the water. This time Samson didn't hesitate. Up to this point, I had no idea where Harry was. I hadn't heard a peep out of him.

Samson apparently decided that I meant business. He turned, loped toward the pool and leaped into the water with a loud splash. I wondered what he would do next. How would he react to being bullied? Would he charge me again and not stop this time. Would his anger toward me overcome his need to eat? Immediately, he resurfaced and looked in my direction. I blew my whistle and threw him a fish. It went straight down to his stomach.

***

Now, the California sea lion prefers smaller pieces of fish. However, with Samson and Delilah, I noticed, they swallowed their fish whole. Later on, I learned that Samson's extraordinary agility and speed enabled him to catch 2-3 pound mackerel thrown like a football. I used to put some heat on my throws — they came furiously fast having played a lot of sandlot football over the years and usually as the quarterback. As long as the throw was within his reach either to one side or the other and even a low "ball," Samson was able to catch it. I always threw the fish head first and so hard that I often imagined it would go right down his throat and out the other end. He rarely missed if my aim was accurate, which it usually was. However, I tried this tack with a grey seal with less than optimum results. I would throw the fish out to them and very close to the visitors who appeared to enjoy the game. One day I threw it just a bit too long. I hit a dignified looking lady in a fur coat, which looked very expensive, right in the chest. I *cringed*! Fortunately, she had a sense of humor and thought it was pretty funny. It was only then I allowed myself to laugh. I was a little more careful after that.

Bob, whom I introduced earlier as the aquarist frequently bitten, had an amusing tactic. Of course, this was before I took him out of handling marine mammals and put him with the fish. I had stressed that *consistency* was extremely important when handling sea lions — particularly when it came to Samson. Bob took this to another level.

He had carefully watched the way I fed Samson and decided it best to imitate me *precisely*. The problem was, he wasn't much of a football player. While he had some heat on his throws with the mackerel, Samson was perplexed that he couldn't catch them. The first one sailed clear across the pool and over the heads of our visitors (to his credit, at least *he* didn't hit anyone). No matter how hard he tried, Samson would watch the fish sail past him. He may have had speed and agility, but he couldn't jump; at least not from a seated position on a rock in the middle of the pool.

***

Back in the pool at the Pribilof exhibit, Samson swallowed his fish even though he still had a confused look on his face. The whistle, it appeared, meant nothing to him — at least at that moment. Would he be able to make the connection?

The whistle is meant to bridge the small time gap between the behavior — that is, what you want him to do — and the reward: the fish. It would let the animal know immediately, that a reward was forthcoming and served to *reinforce* the behavior so it would occur with some consistency. For those of you with experience in this area, I'm sure this seems like an oversimplification, but for the average reader, it should make sense. The whistle can also serve as a reward in itself and let the trainer add a *few* consecutive behaviors — called a *chain behavior* — to occur before the reward.

After eating the fish, Samson cautiously swam up to the edge of the pool and watched intently to see what my reaction was going to be. Ever so slowly he picked his pectoral flipper up out of the water and placed it on the beach. Immediately I said, "No!"

He removed it. I pointed toward the middle of the pool and said, "Pool!" Samson swam away from the beach, and I blew my whistle and threw him a fish. When I turned, I saw Harry standing there behind me stark white. The blood had drained from his face. Later, he told me how happy he was that Samson had charged me. I said, "*Thanks!*"

Before I left the exhibit that day, I was able to maneuver Samson onto to his "seat" by giving him a series of verbal commands. I no longer needed to yell. He made the association of the command and the whistle to the reward and began to look for the fish after only a few tries. He was frighteningly intelligent! Once he climbed onto the rock, I fed him until he was full (within reason—he ate almost 60 pounds!).

Seating him on the rock was another little tidbit of information we gleaned from research. The Steller sea lion couldn't or wouldn't leap head first off of a rock except into the water. They had to turn all the way around and climb down backward. If Samson gave any impression he might do that, we could be through the tunnel and out the door before he got down. We may have had a death wish, but we weren't stupid! Okay, I admit, that may be up for debate. However, that first day of training was a complete success. I had established control over him. *I* was *the beachmaster*. More importantly, I was still alive. At least for the moment.

Chapter Eight

TOO CLOSE FOR COMFORT

As Samson inched closer to the magical age of four, things got a little more interesting. He began to assert himself and challenge me more than ever. He was starting not to take no for an answer. One day late in September, I was standing on *my* rock when Samson made a move on me. This time he didn't stop at the edge of the rock but encroached on it. Since my leg was in the way, I had no choice but to move. Before I knew it, Samson was up almost on top of me, and I had to give up my territory. It wasn't a good sign, and I was uncertain as to what was going on. Fortunately, I remained aggressive toward him, and we had an interchange of sorts. He threw a few head moves at me, and I countered with my little tiny stick.

I thought long and hard about what was happening and decided I better change tactics quickly because, if it came down to a real battle, I would lose. I threw a fish into the pool and yelled to him, "Go!" Samson dove in and retrieved it. I said, "Good!" and threw him another. Then I moved around and gave Samson the command for him to take his seat, which he promptly did. It's a good thing sea lions can't out-think a human!

Or could they?

***

It occurred to me I better get a bigger stick. My guess was that Samson might just be entering puberty. I didn't know where the line between mock fighting and real battles would begin, so I decided on a long bamboo pole, another tactic I learned from research.

Samson's reaction to the pole was instantaneous. I regained control again, and for a couple of weeks, all returned to normal. I even regained control of *my* rock. However, late one afternoon I went out onto the beach to clean. I was just going to hose down the beach as I often did. It was late afternoon, and a crowd was gathering.

Samson acted a little agitated, but I didn't think anything of it. He was watching me and swimming back and forth. I didn't like the look in his eyes and decided the beach was clean enough, and I'd better get out of there. I didn't

have my bamboo pole either.

As I headed back toward the tunnel, Samson quickly swam over ahead of me and jumped out blocking the way. He stood there with fire in his eyes and glared at me. I didn't like this situation at all. There was nowhere for me to go. The top of the wall was a good twenty feet high, and the rocks were flat—too sheer for me to climb. There was no other way out.

Samson was making head bobbing moves and growling. That was a challenge for control of the beach. Since the "harem" comprised of Delilah, I was certainly willing to let him have her. But this wasn't about the harem. It was about who was going to be the beachmaster again.

I got the attention of Pam, one of the attendants who would later become my wife. I remembered one incident that we both laugh about to this day. Samson seemed to enjoy harassing the crowds by roaring at them. In particular, he didn't like some men.

Primarily, he seemed intent on venting this toward *bearded* men. My guess was that his veterinarian in Canada might have had a beard. Sea lions don't seem to take kindly to the individuals who stick them with needles and cause them discomfort despite it being in their best interests.

One day while Pam was giving her tour guide speech, Samson spotted a man he just didn't like, a man with a beard. He leaped up onto his rock island not far from where the visitors were standing and roared with a loud expulsion of deep guttural sounds and air. Along with the roar, however, came a wad of mucous that caught Pam right in her glasses. There she was looking at the crowd with this huge disgusting thing dripping slowly from her glasses. Without missing a beat, she took them off and cleaned them in a nearby stream, turned to Samson and said, "Thanks, Sam." Then she continued giving her guided tour.

That day Pam was the one who responded to my plea for help. She knew I was in big trouble and ran to get help. In the meantime, I stayed behind a large rock. Samson was biding his time. It was as if he knew he had me.

After a few minutes, one of the aquarists came around and asked what they could do. I asked her to get me the bamboo pole and hand it to me from over the top of the roof. When I had the pole in hand, I made my way out from behind the rock. I raised it up, and that should have scared Samson off, but he turned his head away and came at me and lunged. He meant business. *This was no mock battle. Samson intended to win the fight.* I parried, and Samson lunged again. I was holding my end of the beach. He wasn't advancing. I yelled, and he roared.

The crowd had the most bizarre reaction I had ever witnessed. I now know what the people the Romans threw to the lions must have felt. The crowd was yelling, "Kill him! Kill him!" They were not telling me this. They were yelling to Samson to kill *me*! I wonder if they understood that I was in a battle of my life at that moment. How could I ever win against an animal with Samson's size, strength, and agility? To give you some idea of the power that Samson possessed, I offer the following.

***

I remember trying to take a blood sample and performing a physical on Salty, a trained California sea lion. He once picked up a trainer on stage and shook her so hard that it dislocated her shoulder. She decided to "retire" from the business. Salty had been a real star in his day, thrilling audiences at the Aquarium of Niagara Falls before coming here. But Salty had become unpredictable as of late. So he was retired from shows and sent out to our California Coastline exhibit hopefully to breed with one of the several females we had there.

With the smaller sea lions, there wasn't any problem using a squeeze cage when we couldn't train an animal to allow us to draw blood as a trained behavior. However, with Salty, because of his size and unpredictability, we couldn't draw blood or examine him without restraint. We had to use the squeeze cage we used on the young elephant seals to immobilize him. At least, that was the plan.

Samson wasn't in the California Coast exhibit at this point, so we drained the pool and intended on examining all of the animals in the exhibit. It went well, and the cage worked perfectly. We would corral an animal into a corner with boards. There were about eight of us including the veterinarian. We would separate out each animal one at a time and guide it into the squeeze cage. Once in there, the physical lasted for about 5-10 minutes.

Once we had examined all of the animals, it was Salty's turn. He was the largest and most dangerous. We were able to herd him in with little difficulty. Salty barked repeatedly but seemed resigned to his fate. Because of his weight, which was about 450 pounds, we had all of us stand on the squeeze cage and even brought in a few extra bodies from among the attendants to provide additional weight.

Once everyone was in position, we cautioned them to watch their hands and fingers. Then we lowered the bars onto Salty squeezing him to the bottom of the cage. Once we had him in position, something unbelievable happened. Salty *stood up*! Yes, against all of the force we could exert, Salty bent back the bars of the cage like they were made of rubber and walked away.

Everyone jumped back. Salty made no aggressive moves at anyone; he casually walked away and joined the rest of the sea lions huddled in the corner of the pool. He had a look on his face like he did this every day.

We all stood around with our mouths open for a few minutes and gawked. I couldn't believe the sheer power of this animal. I thought about the power that Samson must possess. Samson was over a half ton. Just how much power did *that* animal have if Salty could do this? Samson was an appropriate name.

That's what I was thinking—particularly at that moment on the beach fighting for my life.

***

The battle went on for almost an hour. I even considered the option of having someone drop a ladder down to me and had almost decided that was my only option when Samson seemed to back up some. I took advantage and moved in on him with the bamboo pole and Samson ducked back out of the way, but backed up again. I slowly managed to maneuver him into the water and promptly, I exited. It was a frightening experience. I was quickly running out of ideas on how to control this animal and wondered what we were going to do in the future.

***

Clearly, Samson was again becoming far too dangerous for anyone to work with and it fell to Harry and me again to handle Samson alone. We decided that it was time to arm ourselves with something a little more effective than a bamboo pole. We needed to be able to defend ourselves in the event of an attack.

We came up with the idea of a long, light-weight, *metal* pole. It was about 8 feet long, hollow but made of aluminum. It was light enough for us to handle and, we hoped, could be used to poke him if necessary. I expected that a light tap on his face would let him know we could hurt him. Not really, but we were again going for a psychological advantage.

The next day I went out as usual. The feeding session went without incident. Harry fed next without any problem. Then I tested our weapon under controlled circumstances. Again I went out onto the beach to hose it down. I watched as Samson stalked me from the water. As I turned to leave, he again jumped out ahead of me and cut off my escape. Harry was nearby this time if I needed help.

I advanced on Samson's position with my pole held out in front of me and warned Samson, "No! Pool!" Samson growled at me and lunged with several short feints. I took the edge of the pole and hit him in the chest. It surprised him. He hadn't expected that.

I held the pole over his head as I had done with the bamboo pole and Samson backed down immediately. He seemed to sense that this might hurt him. We regained control as long as we had the pole with us at all times.

And then it happened. It was as close to death as I had ever come!

The Pribilof Islands Exhibit. The infamous tunnel is dead center

Chapter Nine

SAMSON — THE BEACHMASTER!

A young bull challenging the reigning Beachmaster for his harem

The next couple of weeks went well. Samson was spending more and more time chasing Delilah around the pool, but I don't think she was in estrus (heat) yet preparing her for breeding. When that happened, they would mate. One day I came into work early and went out to Seal Island as I routinely did to check up on all of the animals. I walked through on the visitor's side first. It was a cool day with a light rain falling that chilled the bones.

I went into Samson's exhibit after grabbing my pole and walked down to the edge of the beach. Samson was a couple of feet away and bobbing gently in the water with his eyes closed. He appeared so serene. I lowered the tip of my pole and the next thing I knew, Samson was in the air and heading right at me. It was an instantaneous decision. In less time than it takes to blink, I realized Samson *had me*! There was no time to raise the pole for protection. *That* is what I meant earlier when I said that sometimes the rules changed. If I hadn't backed down, Samson would have flattened me like a bucket of fish.

The adrenalin in my body surged, and I ran for my life. I remembered in that split second that a human couldn't outrun a Steller sea lion over rough terrain, but at that moment, I was no ordinary human. I was a human who was about to die, and I believed that with every fiber of my being. I felt Samson's breath on my neck and waited for the sharp pain that would come as he grabbed me. Everything slowed down like a slow motion movie. I didn't have to think about what my body was doing at that moment. It just reacted.

I couldn't remember if I shut the door behind me. If I made it that far and *had* closed it, I'd have been crushed against it. When I reached the end of the tunnel, I found I had left the door open. Miraculously, I made it through the door, and Samson hadn't caught me. Humans *can* outrun a Steller over rough terrain. At least this one did. I grabbed the sliding door as I went through and slammed it as hard as I could at the same instant Samson hit it with all of this weight. The door buckled and nearly came off its hinges.

I was breathing hard. And I was infuriated with Samson for putting me in this predicament. The consummate animal trainer in me kicked back in. I knew what I had to do. If I didn't go back in there and reassert dominance over Samson, we would *never* get back in that exhibit again—ever.

Perhaps that wouldn't have been such a bad thing, but I wasn't exactly thinking clearly at the moment. I looked around for something to use as a weapon. Lying on the ground next to the door was a piece of pipe with an elbow on the end. Someone had been careless while doing some electrical work and left it there. Thankfully! I grabbed it and swung the door open. Samson stood there with a look of surprise on his face. I saw that face once before, the first time I stood up to him that day when Harry and I put our lives on the line to try and train him.

I started screaming at him at the top of my lungs. I called him every nasty name I knew. I insulted his mother, father, and brothers—I cursed and growled all the while swinging the pipe to and fro in front of him hitting the rocks and doorway. It had the desired effect. Samson *ran* from me and dove back into the water. I can't imagine how frightening *I* must have looked to *him*! I glared at him. He looked back with could only be described as a hurt look on his face—as if to say, "What did I do?"

I had every intention of taking out a few teeth if he had charged at me. It wasn't anger so much as fear. Fear that we would have to put Samson down if we couldn't manage him. I walked away from the pool after snarling at Samson and walked up the tunnel that only moments earlier had almost been my grave. I walked through the door and calmly closed and locked it. Then I slid to the ground unconscious. I passed out cold.

***

I couldn't understand what had happened when I came to some several minutes later. I got up and shook off the faintness I felt and walked unsteadily back to the main aquarium building. It pained me that Samson could try so hard to kill me. He wouldn't have stopped. I would learn later on what my fate could have been when we moved Samson into the California Coast exhibit.

Sometime after breeding season when Samson was in the exhibit that disaster struck again. It was then that the elephant seals I mentioned earlier received their bite wounds. Despite all our best efforts, we lost all three of the seals from the wounds Samson inflicted on them. It was a terribly sad time for me. I loved those animals deeply. Some three decades later, I still miss them.

The aggression didn't stop there. Samson chased down a young sea lion pup and eventually wore her down until she became exhausted. What started out as play turned deadly; Samson forced the pup underwater. She drowned. Then he decided to protect the dead pup as his own. It took me the better part of the day to get it away from him.

Not long after that, Samson killed another young sea lion. Then the unbelievable happened. Samson killed a bull California sea lion by the name of Sleepy. Sleepy was no slouch. He weighed in at 650 pounds. Exactly what happened, we had no idea. When I arrived early one morning, Samson was pushing the dead body of Sleepy around the pool. Again he was protecting the carcass as his possession.

I went out onto the beach and tried to position myself to pull the massive sea lion away from him. Samson snarled at me between his teeth. I had my metal pole and was fully prepared to use it on him. I spent the better part of the morning trying to get the poor dead animal away from Samson, but he wasn't having any of it.

It wasn't until later that morning that Samson, while swimming in the middle of the pool, picked up the 650-pound animal and flung it *in the air some fifteen feet* onto the beach. For only a moment I stood there in awe at the strength that must have taken. Then I bolted out onto the beach and got between Samson and Sleepy.

Now the question became what to do with the body? It was far too heavy to drag by myself. Samson was also rushing the beach and trying to get out of the water to get his toy back and deal with me in the process. It was all I could do to keep him in the water. I came up with an idea.

Calling for help, I sent someone to get the Maintenance crew out here as fast as possible with a large cart and rope. Four guys showed up. I asked them to come out on the beach and take Sleepy away. Samson went ballistic when he saw all the strangers wandering about and swam back and forth looking for an opening. I managed to catch him in the mouth with the end of the pole just enough to remind him this wasn't bamboo. That worked.

In the meantime, the maintenance crew was scratching their heads behind me trying to figure out how to get the heavy animal onto the cart. I suggested they put the cart on its side and then tie Sleepy to the cart. Once they had that done, I figured the four of them could push it over.

I tried to impress upon them the seriousness of the situation. They just didn't get it. We were all in mortal danger! Maybe they trusted me. Not such a great idea. I couldn't hold Samson off for much longer. He was highly agitated. If he decided to challenge the metal pole, it wouldn't have stopped him. My control was pure illusion.

Eventually, they followed my instructions and removed Sleepy. However, I now knew how much danger we were in when working with Samson, when I saw how easily, *while in the water*, he had flung that heavy animal so far in the air and onto the beach.

***

Back in the main Aquarium building, all I could think of at the moment was the hot breath on the nape of my neck. I had to fight to keep from fainting again.

I went into the office in the main building where Jeff, my supervisor, and I had our desks. There were a couple of more desks for the aquarists and a long table for meetings. The clipboard with the entries hung on the wall next to the cork bulletin board with various notes. I looked through them but saw nothing that indicated anything unusual about Samson. Harry would certainly have left me a note.

I scanned the chart down to "Pribilof exhibit." There was an entry by *Jeff,* my supervisor. Why was Jeff making entries in the log, I wondered? Wouldn't Harry have made the entries? I read on.

The log said, "Delilah looks too thin. Tried to feed. Left when Samson became aggressive."

Jeff tried to feed Delilah? Why would he do that? Harry and I had made the decision not to worry. The females often stopped eating when they went into estrus. The literature indicated that this happens in nature and so we weren't concerned. It would only last for a short time. Even Samson would stop eating for a while. He didn't have a current weight at this point, but we estimated him close to 1200 pounds. Delilah likely had begun the season around 700 pounds but could drop 200 with little concern. It was normal. Our VP was well aware of the situation, and we had his approval. Jeff should have stayed out of it. I couldn't understand why he wouldn't have just let Harry handle it.

I noticed there were no entries at all by Harry. That seemed peculiar. We *always* made some comment about the day to alert the other, especially when the other person would be off. It was Harry's day on—at least I thought it was.

I went over to look at the schedule and was horrified to discover that Harry and I were *both* scheduled to be off yesterday! *How had that happened? Why didn't Jeff call and let us know? What had he done that caused Samson to attack me like that?* Then it occurred to me. I knew in my heart what had happened and I was *furious* with Jeff. At that moment I didn't care if he was my supervisor or not. I had come as close to death as I ever want to. It didn't make me feel alive — it frightened me.

I stormed around looking for anything to vent my anger. No one was around yet. I walked out to Seal Island to the Pribilof exhibit and looked in on Samson from the visitor's side of the exhibit.

A cold wind chilled me and I shook both from the wind and the adrenalin that was probably still in my veins. Samson was trying to mount Delilah in the water. Well, that wasn't going to work. She kept biting him in the face, but it only seemed to make him more aggressive. Still she resisted. We could no longer go into the exhibit until breeding season had ended. Neither of them was going to eat anyway.

***

Around 9:00 AM Jeff came into the office. I was waiting for him sipping a cup of coffee that tasted too bitter. It was probably my attitude.

"What the heck happened yesterday with Sam?" I screamed at him. Jeff was taken aback.

"You better back off, John. Next time show up when you're supposed to!"

"Someone screwed up the schedule. That wasn't supposed to happen!"

Now I was on the defensive. That wasn't my plan. I remembered the breath on the nape of my neck. "Why didn't you call me? Or Harry! We would have come in!"

"I did call, but you weren't home; neither was Harry!" Now Jeff was on the defense.

"Then, why did you go into the exhibit? No one, including you, should have gone in there."

"I was worried about Delilah. I decided she was looking thin. I thought I'd try and feed her a few fish. She looked hungry."

"And Samson attacked you, didn't he? You *ran* from him, right?" I accused.

"I didn't think he would do that. I ran before he got too close."

"Do you know what almost happened this morning? *I almost got killed!* Do you realize what you did by running? You set up a predator-prey response behavior in him. You can *never* run from an animal like that. It set me up for the attack. He saw me as *prey!* He almost caught me this morning."

"Oh, so you can run from him and I can't? Is that it? I obviously didn't do anything you didn't do. You just said that *you* ran from him!"

"I...I...what's the use. You just don't get it!"

I stormed out of the office. I always used to let anger get the better of me, and I couldn't talk when that happened. Over the years I learned to control it. However, that day I clearly lost control. I'm sure Jeff meant well and his concern was for the animals. Jeff was a *brilliant* man, but sometimes logic failed him. I, on the other hand, wasn't so bright. My formal education was sorely lacking, but I was a logical, creative thinker. That day I struggled to stay in touch with my logical sense.

I called Harry since I knew he was in and explained what had just happened that morning. We both agreed that staying out of the exhibit until the breeding urges subsided was a good idea. Harry also agreed with my assessment of the scenario that had almost gotten me killed. Jeff and I apologized to one another. That night we went out to dinner at a Chinese restaurant in Uncasville. The sign outside always drove me crazy. It read "restau*rat*", but the food was pretty good.

My meal came and I began eating; the Pu Pu platter with lots of fried rice seasoned with MSG. Suddenly, without warning, I was overcome with a tremendous sense of panic. It was the kind of panic I had felt a few times as a youngster when trapped in closed in spaces. It was like the time one of my brothers and I had hidden in the trunk of my father's car while living on Spring St. in New London, Connecticut where I grew up.

I panicked — to the amusement of my trapped brother Alan who didn't seem fazed by this at all. Tommy, another of my brothers, responded to the banging of my fist and screaming. Alan just laughed all the more. Tommy, in his haste, had broken the key off and we were trapped. He ran and got my father who managed to get the key out somehow. He had a backup key and released us. It was many years before I was able to control my claustrophobia. That night in the restaurant, the panic returned with a vengeance.

I ran out of the restaurant to the embarrassment of my wife and friends. I stood outside hyperventilating and made the panic all the worse. We left the restaurant before anyone ate. I felt bad about that. On the ride home I calmed myself down and reasoned it was a latent response to Samson's attack. In the weeks ahead I would wake up soaked with perspiration pouring off my forehead as I felt the breath on the nape of my neck in my nightmares.

Chapter Ten

WINTER

At least someone likes winter!

Winter always presented a challenge to feeding the marine mammals outside. Winds, rain, snow, blizzards and hurricanes didn't stop us from caring for our seals and sea lions. Occasionally, we wound up staying all night at the Aquarium after working through the day. I was at the Aquarium when the "Blizzard of 78" hit the east coast (okay, so I'm old!).

We watched the storm progress on the news as the day went on and ran around like the proverbial chicken with their heads cut off (where on earth did we come up with such colorful sayings?). A handful of us stayed to get all of the animals fed and made sure that everything that could be tied down was tied down, or anything that could blow away was secured. The local weather (this is BC — Before the Weather Channel) indicated it was going to be bad: high winds near hurricane force and blinding snow.

None of us particularly wanted to stay at the Aquarium all night, and we raced to get all our work done. We fed everyone a little extra just in case we didn't make it in the next day. It was around noon that the first flakes began to fall.

There were four of us left. Everyone else had headed out and made it home well before the storm hit. By the time we finished, the winds had picked up considerably. It was late afternoon and getting dark out.

Finally, we finished and ran out to our cars. However, the snow buried our cars in snow drifts so high we couldn't open the doors. We knew right then we'd be spending the night. Great. We hadn't had lunch, and the only thing on the menu was raw fish! I didn't even like sushi!

By this time, I had been promoted to Curator when Jeff took a position at a zoo in another state. As Curator of Exhibits, it fell to me to make the final decision. I called the General Manger of the Aquarium and asked her if the Aquarium would foot the bill if we all stayed at the Ramada Inn just down the street. We said we could easily walk there and we were all famished. I threw in the idea that we could be back at the Aquarium first thing in the morning so we could take care of all the fish! She took the bait (sorry, I couldn't help myself).

By the time we headed out, it was dark. The wind was howling through the electrical wire and telephone poles. We dressed with everything we could find. There was no shortage of winter gear when you work year round at an Aquarium!

The Ramada Inn was a short walk down Coogan Boulevard and then maybe a quarter mile up Route 27. On a good day, we often went there for lunch—a short walk of fifteen minutes. Not that the customers liked us very much.

One day a few of us went there for lunch. We walked past a table, and some regal looking older lady exclaimed, "What on earth is that horrible smell!" One of our aquarists stopped and looked at her and, without losing a beat said, "You don't smell too hot yourself, lady!" Is it any wonder why so many people ordered fish at MacDonald's whenever we ate there?

The walk down Coogan Blvd. wasn't too bad. The wind wasn't directly hitting us. However, when we turned the corner to go up Route 27, the full force of the blizzard bore down. Snow pelted us in the face so badly we had to walk backward. There were no cars on the road. In fact, we couldn't even tell where the road was!

Two of my colleagues started going up the ramp toward I-95 convinced it was the right direction. I staunchly refused to follow them and was convinced they were wrong, but told them if that's where they wanted to go, it was their choice. They decided I just might be right. Fortunately, I was. Even in the storm, my nose knew where to get food and a warm bed.

The infamous Blizzard of '78

When we arrived at the Ramada some sixty minutes later, we encountered a slap-happy group of people stranded like ourselves. The management was extremely cooperative and gave us discounts on everything. Anything they had on hand to eat was at our disposal. It turned into quite a party. We were *much* happier at the hotel than we would have been had we stayed and gnawed on herring sushi and slept on the concrete floor.

When we awoke late the next morning, the sun was shining, and the plows were just starting to make a dent in the huge mounds of drifting snow. We walked back without any problem and were considered heroes for having stayed through the blizzard. If they only knew.

***

The winter presented another problem with slick beaches. I came close to another Samson disaster because of some ice on the beach one day. Samson was in the California Coast exhibit, and it was the dead of winter. It had rained the day before, and then the temperature plummeted during the night — a common occurrence in New England. It was the kind of day when your breath looked like the exhaust spewing from a Mac truck trying to get up a steep hill. The plows had been out all night sanding to prevent cars from skidding off the road.

I arrived early — as usual — and had several cups of coffee. After donning a heavy parka and fur-lined rubber gloves, I headed out the large sliding door and tunnel leading to the exhibit. Samson was already on his seat at the base of the tunnel and vocalizing. He was obviously hungry. It was the winter after we lost the elephant seals. Sam's aggression was still prominent although not as marked as earlier in the season.

I always dreaded what would happen if I were to go into the water with Samson. I had been swimming with sand tiger sharks, California sea lions, dolphins, whales and harbor seals. However, I felt I would have as much chance swimming with Samson as with a great white shark in the open ocean. I would rather jump from a plane without a parachute. I had heard of people surviving that scenario. I had no hope of surviving an encounter in the water with Samson.

It was those kinds of thoughts that were racing through my mind as I stepped into the tunnel and lost my footing. It was solid ice all the way down. Just to the left of Samson (my right), there was a small haul-out area that dipped into the pool. I was sliding quickly toward it. I lost the steel bucket full of fish as it slid along with me and clawed at the ground with my hands and feet trying desperately to keep from slipping into the water dead ahead of me.

***

Back when Samson and Delilah were in the Pribilof exhibit, I realized the dangers of controlling such a beast as Sammy. On one occasion, we were hosing down some algae from the public side of the exhibit before it was open to the public. Someone dropped the hose down a small opening in one of the rocks and went to do something else. The hose was dangling into the pool. Samson saw it, got curious and swam up to the hose. He moved his vibrissae back and forth across the hose to see what it was. Their whiskers, called *vibrissae* are extraordinarily sensitive.

We once had inherited a totally blind sea lion from another facility by the name of Ginger. Ginger was quite old and, at one time, had been a performing sea lion although I can't recall where. Ginger could catch fish thrown to her from 6 feet away as long as it hit the vibrissae. I wondered just how sensitive they were one day and did something that could have gotten me severely bitten. But I was going on a hunch.

I called out to Ginger, and the vibrissae flared forward. Then I threw her a fish. I did it again. Then I called her name and quickly shoved my bare hand into her vibrissae. Her mouth bounced off my hand, but her mouth never opened!

Well, Samson was using his vibrissae to determine what the unusual thing was dangling in his pool and spewing water. Suddenly, he reached out and grabbed the hose and raced off across the pool with it. When I saw that happen, I was horrified! *"What if some little child had struck his or her hand down in that crevice?"*

Sometimes it was the parents who concerned us. Seriously, what parent would hang their child over the enclosure of a dangerous animal? Okay, the Crocodile Hunter aside, we continually worried about the parents that placed their children on the wall to get a better look. Samson had the ability to leap above the glass and railing enclosing the exhibit. Then the unbelievable happened.

One morning I made my way out to Seal Island early for my rounds. I made sure that everything was functioning normally, the animals were all okay, and the exhibits were ready for viewing. It was a beautiful cool, crisp, clear day. I had my coffee, and I enjoyed this time alone with the animals away from the screaming crowds. Really, people, do you have any idea how silly you look and sound making seal and sea lion noises?

I casually strolled around the corner past the California Coast exhibit to the Pribilofs. There was a small concrete section of wall between two large, monolithic rocks where the visitors could get an unusual view of the exhibit. You could see behind some the boulders and up the tunnel, and there was an area the animals could get out and explore.

As I came around the corner, Samson was *sitting on top of the wall of the exhibit.* It was so surrealistic; at first, I didn't comprehend what I saw.

I said, "Good morning, Sam!" I kept walking for a few steps. *Then* it hit me. I turned with a look of complete horror on my face, and there was Samson with a look on *his* face like I just caught him in the cookie jar!

I reacted, at this point, by racing at him and screaming. Samson lost his balance and fell backward into the pool with a loud splash. I shut the exhibit down and requested the Maintenance Department install a stainless steel railing around the inside of the exhibit at an angle to prevent Samson from climbing or getting near the children people placed on the walls. And to keep him *in* the enclosure. Now you know where I got the idea for my novel!

***

Now back to my morning sleigh ride. As I slid down the tunnel clawing at the ice, I seemed to be picking up speed. Samson watched somewhat confused, or maybe he was just a little bemused. Apparently, he had never seen anyone enter the exhibit like this before.

I, on the other hand, was panic stricken! One heavy boot hit the water. If I went in, I would have sunk right to the bottom. My parka and boots would have prevented me from getting back out. Samson would have gone in and…I shudder to think what would have happened.

Somehow (and to this day I don't know), I managed to swing my body against the rock where Samson sat. I looked up at Samson. He looked down at me completely befuddled. I got up, grabbed the bucket and began feeding him. I tried very hard not to think about what had almost happened just then, but from that day on, you can be sure I kept a bucket of salt near the door to spread on icy cold days!

***

One day when Samson was in the California Coast exhibit, I got the bright idea to teach him how to dive off the cliff. I had done this with a California sea lion named Squirty…well, sort of. In their natural environment, sea lions seem to enjoy diving off of rock ledges, so, I decided I would train Squirty to dive off the ten-foot-high cliff in our California Coastline exhibit. The water depth at the base of the cliff was about eight feet. Part of Squirty's repertoire when he was a performer was diving from a bench into the Marine Theater pool from a seat only a couple of feet high. However, we wondered: would he jump into the pool from ten feet?

A California sea lion about Squirty's age and size.

I was dressed in a bathing suit and prepared to dive in along with Squirty if necessary. Always have a plan, right? It had more to do with finding an excuse to go swimming with the sea lions (by the way, Samson wasn't in here at this point. I'm crazy, not suicidal). There were about a dozen or so other sea lions in the pool, but they typically ignored you unless you had a bucket of fish in your hand. I had been in the pool with them before. They liked to swim by at a phenomenal rate of speed, bounce off my SCUBA tank and scare me half to death.

The first dive Squirty performed went off without a hitch. He was trained to assume a handstand on his front flippers balancing himself with absolute perfection at the edge of the cliff. He held his rear flippers up over his head with a beautiful arching form. Squirty could even shift his weight of 300 pounds to one flipper and catch rings on his head thrown to him from several feet away — and this while balancing a ball on the end of his nose at the same time!

I gave the appropriate vocal command, "Go!" and pointed in the direction of the pool. Squirty leaped forward straight down into the pool and, instead of gliding skillfully into the water, he landed with a loud splat. It was a less than perfect belly flop.

I quickly reinforced the behavior and rewarded him with several fish right away hoping to keep him from being discouraged. I led him back up the stairway to the cliff area that consisted of carefully placed rock ledges leading to the top. Squirty followed and even appeared eager — but not with as much enthusiasm as previously.

I ran him through a few other behaviors to relax him and take his mind off the previous jump. A large crowd had gathered to watch with interest the drama unfolding in the exhibit.

"Squirty!" I said playing to the crowd. What can I say? There has always been a little ham in me from playing in rock bands when I was in high school. He looked at me expectantly.

"Are you ready?"

Squirty shook his head up and down enthusiastically. No, he didn't *really* have a clue what I was asking. The response was to a very subtle hand signal from the end of my finger that the crowd couldn't see. Oh, I can be so sneaky sometimes!

"Are you sure you're ready?"

Squirty vocalized loudly, "Ahhhhhhh!" and then shook his head again. I had combined two hand signals this time: one for the vocalization and the other for the headshake.

"Okay, Squirty, *up!*" Squirty immediately assumed his beautiful flipper stand. I gave the signal with a sweep of my arm and yelled, "Go!"

Squirty got down from his handstand and looked at me with a blank expression on his face. To save face, I hammed it up again.

"I thought you were ready to try again?" Squirty shook his head no this time—in response to yet another hand signal.

"Are you ready to try again?" Squirty shook his head up and down. Yep, a hand signal.

"Okay, Up!" Squirty struck his pre-dive pose with less of an arch than previously. "Go!"

Squirty got down again and looked at me. Was he *trying* to make a fool out of me? Probably not intentionally. But we had an audience! I was going to make the best of this show one way or another.

"Aren't you going to go for me?"

Squirty shook his head.

"Please?"

Again he shook his head.

"You should be *ashamed* of yourself!"

Squirty bowed his head and put a flipper over his eyes. The crowd let out an audible, "Awwwwww." The word *ashamed* said with emphasis was the vocal command for this behavior. The crowd was applauding now. They were eating it up!

"Do you want me to show you how to do it?"

Squirty nodded.

I had an assistant standing by on the beach below. I threw the bucket to her and then dove off the cliff. The water was cold and took my breath away for a second. I swam to a small cluster of rocks near the base of the cliff and got out. My assistant threw the bucket to me, and I continued to converse with Squirty.

"Now, do you see how it's done?"

Head nod.

"It's easy, isn't it?"

Another head nod.

"Okay, now *you* do it."

Squirty shook his head no.

"What d'ya chicken?"

Head nod.

"You should be ashamed of yourself."

Head down and flipper over the eyes.

"Well, I forgive you." Head back up and vocalizations. The crowd was applauding. I think they believed I was carrying on a conversation with Squirty. I felt a little guilty and turned and explained to the crowd what had transpired. It would have been unfair if I let them believe that Squirty had understood what I was saying. We made an effort to teach our visitors about natural behaviors and trained behaviors avoiding the anthropomorphizing attitude shown by some in the industry. These are magnificent creatures, and we felt it undignified to present them as trained clowns.

***

I had something slightly different in mind with Samson. There was no way I was going to go up to the top *with* him, let alone jump in the pool to show him how to do it. Samson was smart—*really* smart. I hoped to convince him through a series of hand signals and verbal commands what I wanted him to do.

I also took a play from the dolphins' playbook. No, not the *Miami* Dolphins football team! When trainers wanted to get a dolphin to jump, they begin by having the dolphin "target" on a ball at the end of a long aluminum pole. Then, gradually, the dolphin will get the idea he or she has to jump to touch the ball to get a reward: a fish.

Since Samson was already trained to target on a ball, I used the same technique to, first of all, get Samson to climb up the ledge on command. By reaching out from a safe place on the beach, I had Samson "follow the bouncing ball" up to the top. Once there, I had him target on the ball, and then I made an arching move with it toward the water. At the same time, I said pool and followed with a hand command pointing to the water.

Samson watched in, what I can only describe as, enthusiastic fascination. He *liked* to learn new things. He looked at me and then at the water, thought about it and then lay on his stomach and tried to reach down to the water. I have to give him credit for effort. Nice try, but it wasn't what I was wanted.

I threw a fish into the water and, of course, one of the California sea lions raced over to gobble it down. Now I had a crowd of animals gathered under the ledge, but I also had Samson's attention. Nothing like a little friendly competition.

I gave the command again followed by a sweeping motion with the pole and pointed to the water. "Pool!"

This time Samson leaped off the edge of the cliff. He plummeted to the bottom and landed about as ungracefully as I've ever seen an animal hit the water—except maybe Squirty. Apparently, this isn't as natural as everyone thought it was.

Water flew out in every direction and soaked me. "Thanks, Samson!" But I really didn't mind. I blew my whistle and threw fish after fish to reward him. I was ecstatic! I only hoped that the thunderous belly flop wouldn't deter him from trying again.

I gave him a command and pointed to the ledge. Samson went up without much problem. He came to the edge of the ledge and looked down. I could swear there was a look of fear in his eyes. I gave the command as before. "Pool!"

Samson lay down and, with a pathetic sounding growl, he looked at me. It was clear that he had gone the way of Squirty. I had gotten him to dive, but I was the only one who saw it happen. No one ever believed he did it.

The California Coastline Exhibit with the "diving platform" dead center.

Chapter Eleven

LOOKING BACK

It has been over thirty years now that Samson has been gone. Sometimes it seems like yesterday. Of all the animals I ever worked with, none ever had the impact that Samson did. He taught me a great deal about myself. He humbled me with his power, agility, and intelligence. I learned how puny humans can be and how tenuous our control on the world around us.

As I look back on my career working in a public aquarium, a part of me is sad that we have to take these magnificent creatures out of their beautiful homes and place them in cement enclosures for our enjoyment. There are many arguments we can use to justify keeping them in captivity. I know — I've used them all. However, when I am honest with myself, I am faced with some difficult questions.

Take Samson, for instance. It had taken all of those mistakes, deaths of other animals, and nearly a few of our own lives before we got it through our thick skulls that we didn't have the ability to handle him in captivity. As natural as they seemed, it was still an artificial environment and produced artificial, abnormal behaviors in the animals. Samson was an animal whose natural instincts dictated he fight for survival. All our efforts to modify that instinctive programming failed. The small measure of successes we had wasn't worth the dangers.

The summer Samson turned five; he was still in the California Coast exhibit. Finally, breeding season had passed, and the aggression ebbed. I knew in my heart we couldn't go through another breeding season. The odds of someone getting severely injured or killed would grow greater the following season.

I got a call that the benefactor of the Mystic Aquarium was coming for a visit. His name was Mr. Smith. To this day that's all I ever really knew about him; that, and he was a very wealthy man who loved the sea and the creatures in it.

Whenever he visited, he always stopped and asked me to tell him how the animals were doing—by name. He was up in years, frail and needed a cane to get about. One of the things he was most interested in was Samson. I later found out Mr. Smith was the one who made the deal to get Samson for us.

Part of my job involved exhibit design and construction and one that I learned I had an aptitude. When we first started building the aquarium, I was hired as a laborer to construct and build all of the aquarium exhibits and, eventually, Seal Island. That training came in handy.

I had an idea. In the front entrance to the Aquarium off to the left was a small section of concrete pond (remember the one where the grey seals went out for long passes with the mackerel? And where I hit the woman in the fur coat?). One of my favorite things next to working with the animals themselves was designing and building the exhibits. I decided I was going to design an exhibit exclusively for Samson.

I sketched out my idea and took measurements. I wanted Samson nose to nose with the visitors so he could roar and fling "snark" (what we affectionately called the forceful discharges from his nose and throat) at the people he didn't like in complete safety.

The key to the exhibit's success was an unusual moat around it. It was a dry moat whose walls leaned slightly in at an angle near the top. Samson could go down into the moat and get back up if he wanted, but it was too tall for him to reach anyone and too steep an angle to climb. However, when he stood at the edge of the enclosed pool at the top of the moat, he was only a few feet from the visitors.

I also designed a small house for him to enter that doubled as a squeeze cage. He would be trained to go in there, and we could take blood samples and give him medicines if needed. Escape routes and animal seats were all placed for the safety of the handlers. It was perfect! All we needed was a few bucks from Mr. Smith. I needed to impress him. Actually, it was Samson that needed to impress Mr. Smith.

A couple of days before Mr. Smith's arrival, Samson was acting strange...stranger than normal. He was extremely lethargic and refused to eat. He swam slowly in patterns and wouldn't even look at me. I knew something was wrong, but there was nothing I could do. Had I gotten him to eat, I would have started him on antibiotics as a precaution. Unfortunately, with seals and sea lions, usually the first sign of illness is they stop eating, and a regimen of antibiotics was one of the few recourses we had to treat him.

I knew the solution to the problem was close at hand. But I needed to show Mr. Smith what I had trained Samson to do. I needed to demonstrate his repertoire of "tricks." I was sweating bullets. How was I going to pull this off with Mr. Smith on his way? We desperately needed the money.

Mr. Smith arrived and made his usual visits with the animals but what he really wanted to see was Samson. The elderly gentleman made his way around to the visitor's side. We closed the exhibit for him.

I patiently waited until all the other sea lions were in position and then began giving commands along with an assistant. Everywhere you looked there was a sea lion doing something on command. Sometimes it could be very stressful. If you ignored one of them for what they perceived to be too long, they left their seat and created havoc by invading the other animals' territory.

I called to Samson. He hadn't responded to me in two days. I was extremely concerned about his health. Imagine my surprise when Samson stopped swimming and came over to the haul-out area next to his seat. He looked pathetic. A low grumbling vocalization came out of Samson's mouth, and he just looked at me with what I can only describe as pleading eyes. I knew he was hurting.

I slapped the seat and asked him gently, "Come on, boy. Come on Sam. Up on your seat."

Mentally, I was willing him to come up. Samson swam away from the beach a little distance. Mr. Smith was watching with a childlike intensity and awe.

Then Samson pulled himself up onto the rock with tremendous effort and took his position. He laid down on the rock with his massive flippers hanging pendulously off to each side. I offered him a fish, but he just ignored it. Then I reached out and began to gently stroked him on his head — something we were never supposed to do because it was too easy for him to bite. I sensed I was in no danger. Samson was clearly ill and — if we didn't get the money to build him a new exhibit — I feared for his life.

Mr. Smith was so deeply impressed with me stroking Samson's head; he gave us the money to build the exhibit. His generosity moved me deeply. It is rare to meet a man with so much influence so down to earth. He always remembered my name and the name of all the animals. What a wonderful gentleman.

***

After Mr. Smith had left, I shut the exhibit down and brought the crane back in. It was time to move Samson back into the small enclosure he had been in when he first arrived. He was sick, and it was the only place we had even a chance of medicating him.

The move went off without a hitch. Samson was in no mood or condition to give us any trouble. After a couple of days, he still wasn't eating and spending a lot of time on the platform instead of in the water. I decided to try and give him an injection with a pole syringe. It was going to take over 50 cc's of antibiotic to treat him even once. The syringe had to go deep enough to reach muscle. If left in the blubber, it wouldn't do any good.

I found the strongest 5-inch needle available and filled the syringe. Sammy was sleeping quietly with his body not far from the fence. I snuck up and plunged the needle into him. He roared and jumped up knocking the needle out. Only about 10 cc's made it in at all, and I was pretty sure I didn't get it deep enough. After that, he wouldn't come anywhere near the fence. Boy, did I feel bad.

In the meantime, work began almost immediately on the new exhibit. The check cleared (of which I had no doubt) and it was expected to take around two months to complete. It was an awfully long time to keep Samson and Delilah in that small enclosure.

Another two days passed without Samson eating. I was stumped. I hoped he had enough blubber on him to last. Unfortunately, the news came on my day off.

One of the aquarists arrived at our home in Stonington Village with the sad news. She had tears in her eyes, and I knew right away. I fought back the tears the way a man is supposed to do, but inside it hurt deeply. I had grown exceptionally close to Samson. I had broken my own rule of becoming attached to an animal in captivity. Samson was more than an animal to train. He was a friend.

I dressed and went in and organized the removal of Samson's body. It was difficult maintaining my composure, but no one was the wiser except the people closest to me.

A new Head Curator arrived recently, and we didn't see eye to eye on much. I didn't mind having the help, but, as can happen in any work situation, there was tension about where the boundaries lie between my responsibilities and his.

I had assisted in virtually every necropsy (what we call an autopsy in animals) of every animal that had ever died at the aquarium. The new Head Curator said to me, "John, I want you to go down and assist in Samson's necropsy. Help the veterinarian."

I responded, "I can't do that. Not this time. I just can't…"

"I *order* you to go down there and help with that necropsy…or else!"

"Or else what?"

"Or…else you're fired!"

This particular man had a Ph.D. in Molecular Genetics. I didn't know what that meant at the time, but he seemed to lack even the most fundamental understanding of biology. Whenever I had to explain something to him, I had to break it down into surprisingly simple detail, or he wouldn't get it. *And here I didn't even have a college degree at the time!*

I won't go into all of the things this man did that set me on edge. If he had been an employee, I would have fired *him*. While he wasn't supposed to be my supervisor, he was in charge of the Aquarium's animals over me. I never did figure out how that was supposed to work.

Now here he was threatening to fire me. Why? Because I refused to cut my favorite animal into pieces so we could figure out what happened. When it finally came down to him following through, he backed down. I told him to go ahead and fire me because there was no way I was going to do it.

As it turned out, I did go down there after the necropsy was almost complete. I wanted to see for myself why Samson had died. I wanted to know if there was anything I could have done differently.

It turned out he had chronic pneumonia. It probably had been there all along for some time. Under the circumstances, there was nothing we could have done. He would have had to eat to get the medicine.

***

I learned a great deal working at the Aquarium. Coming so close to death, I learned to embrace life. I also learned that, if we survive the challenges life throws at us, we have no choice but to respond. Either that, or we become nothing, and our life becomes meaningless—just along for the ride.

I never feared anyone or anything after having withstood the challenge of the Beachmaster. It made me tougher. It taught me that whatever goals I set for myself I could reach—if I really wanted that goal badly enough.

My hope is that someday I'll be able to study all of the creatures of the oceans in their natural environment. I want to swim with the dolphins and whales, dive on the magnificent corals of the Great Barrier Reef, and walk among the Steller sea lions as the Beachmaster defends his home. I'll give him a wide berth. I will not challenge him or take him away from his home. I will simply stand aside, watch, and be amazed.

I will do these things—someday. As long as there is a clean earth left to do them in. There will be—if all of us learn to respect the animals on this planet. Someday—there won't be any aquariums or zoos, cages or cement pools. Someday, all the animals will live in peace in their natural environments.

Someday.

Steller sea lions at home on the rookery

Afterword

As I mentioned in my Author's Foreword, the Steller sea lion is an endangered species (at least one population of two; the other threatened). Humans, as a species, bear the responsibility as caretakers of this planet to manage the wild populations of animals in a conscientious manner. We have not always done that although there are organizations on earth whose sole purpose is to right some of the wrongs that greed has wrought on earth's animal kingdom. A commendable part of that responsibility involves education. Following is a short natural history of the Steller sea lion and several resources to that end.

Additionally, I have committed a percentage of the sales of this and future publications of "True Animal Stories" to assist in the rescue of our marine animals. The Mystic Aquarium has an excellent rescue program with a strong track record from the time I was employed there to the present.

I know personally from experience that **the vast majority of animal handlers and trainers care deeply for the animals in their care.** Please give them your support and understanding regardless of how you feel about keeping these creatures in captivity. Working along with them rather than against them benefits in the further education of the general populace about the magnificent animals with which we share the planet.

The Steller Sea Lion—a Natural History

The Steller sea lion (*Eumetopias jubatus*) is the largest of all the sea lions. Sea lions, in general, differ from the "true seals" in several distinct ways. Sea lions belong to the family *Otariidae* while the true seals are members of the *Phocidae*.

Otariids (sea lions) verses Phocids (seals)

The sea lion, including Stellers, have external ear flaps while the seals do not. The seals have a tympanic membrane covering their internal ear. Seals cannot walk on their hind flippers the way the sea lions can since the sea lions have a hinged hip joint. Seals tend to undulate like a giant worm when on land but are quite agile and fast underwater.

Sea lions have long front flippers with which they use to propel themselves through the water and can run on them with their hind flippers on land. Especially is the Steller quick on land and is said to outrun a human over the rough terrain of the rookery.

Breeding

The male Steller is called a bull while the female a cow. One male will set up an area of a beach or rocky outcropping and protect a group of females known as a harem. The bull is known as a beachmaster. The entire population is referred to as a rookery. Younger males frequently challenge the beachmaster for control of the harem and the right to breed; battles can become fierce. The "loser" may breed with any female that wanders away from the harem or has to wait until the following season and try again.

Females breed once a year and have one pup. Fertilization is yearly with delayed implantation of the zygote (the fertilized egg) occurring after three months while the female may be at sea eating and gaining weight for the following season of whelping and breeding.

Males may reach sexual maturity as early as 3-years-old and live to 20. Females may be 3 when mature and live until 30 years, but may not begin breeding on the rookery until later.

Sexual Dimorphism

Males are considerably larger the females and females have a marked size difference. Males may weigh up to 1250 pounds and a length from the tip of the nose to the caudal flippers of 11 feet. They stop growing by the time they are 11. Males are darker in color than the females and develop a ruddy color around their thick necks. Their blubber layer may be 6" thick at peak weight. The head is large and prominent, very distinctive compared to the female.

Females may weigh up to 700 pounds and reach a length of 9'. They are much more slender than the males with a sleek body and more narrow face. Females can grow up to 6 years, and the weight can vary significantly during breeding and whelping season. Female coloration is lighter than the male and ranges from a buff to a silvery coat from year to year.

The Pups and their care

The pups at birth have a dense almost black fur with white-like "frost" since the hair is colorless at the tip. The color eventually lightens late in the season when they "molt" or shed their baby coat.

The pups mature quickly feeding on the calorie dense milk from their mothers. Pups can recognize their mothers' voice when separated such as when the mother swims off to feed. The rookery can be a cacophony of barks, roars, and lamb-like baying when all of the females have given birth. Although they may suckle for three years, they wean after the first. The weight at birth is around 50 pounds.

Diet

Steller sea lions feed on a diet of fishes and cephalopods (squid) and the occasional bird. Mackerel, herring, salmon and pollock are among the fish that constitutes part of their diet. These fish are high in fatty acids providing the dense concentration of calories needed for the sea lions in this frigid environment.

Migration

According to the Alaska Department of Fish and Game, "Sea lions do not migrate, but do move their 'central-place haulout,' the center of their foraging activity, to track seasonal concentrations of their many types of prey. They breed on exposed, offshore rookeries during summer and generally move to more protected haulouts in winter, especially in southeastern Alaska. Very young sea lions can swim 75 miles (120 km) non-stop between haulouts. Some sea lions make long-distance movements over long periods of time. The longest recorded movements are Forrester Island to Cape Newenham (1,600 miles / 2,500 km), Kozlov Cape, Russia to Round Island (1,400 miles / 2,300 km) and Medny Island, Russia to Round Island (1,200 miles / 2,000 km)."

Natural Behavior

Steller males can become extremely aggressive during breeding season, adaptation that allows for the stronger animals to breed and procreate leading to stronger breeding stock. The females become submissive during breeding as they enter estrus (heat) preparing for ovulation although they can hold their own against the males when not in estrus.

Younger males may challenge the beachmaster to territorial battle and, in due time, unseat the reigning animal.

Stellers are well adapted to life on the rookery and in the ocean; swimming with their powerful front flippers, they can propel themselves gracefully through the water and turn quickly to avoid aggressive fish such as the Great White shark or mammal such as the Killer Whale (Orca).

Male Stellers have excellent balance although perhaps not as agile as their California sea lion counterparts. They have the ability to climb vertical cliffs making them difficult to house in captivity since they can escape enclosures that do not account for that ability.

Pups learn to swim in the shallows and quickly learn to dive and forage for fish after their first year. Pups must fast when the mothers venture out to replenish their fat stores which may take up to 2 days.

Habitat

Steller sea lions inhabit rookeries along the North Pacific rim from Japan to east along the Aleutian chain. From there they range into the central Bering Sea, through the Gulf of Alaska, and south through southeastern Alaska, the Canadian Pacific coast and to the Channel Islands off California (Alaska Department of Fish and Game).

Female Steller sea lions generally return to the same breeding sites from year-to-year.

Current Status

Under the Endangered Species Act, Steller sea lions were listed as threatened. Scientists at that time determined that there were two genetically distinct populations. They created two populations based on location, West, and East of 144° longitude. Those to the east of that longitude were considered "endangered" while those in the West recovered and were listed as "threatened."

To determine the cause of the decline in population, scientists studied the animals in their natural environment. According to the Alaska Department of Fish and Game, "...there is substantial effort being made to identify causes for and remedies to the Western stock population decline, and these are the subject of considerable debate. The possible sources of the decline being examined are grouped into "top-down" processes, such as predation, disturbance, intentional killing and entanglements, and "bottom-up" processes, such as reduced prey quality or abundance and long-term shifts in their environment. Assessment of these threats and planning for the recovery of Steller sea lions is a long-term collaborative process involving numerous stakeholder groups. One-fifth of one percent of Steller sea lions sighted during surveys in southeastern Alaska become entangled in marine debris including packing straps and fishing gear, but the extent of mortality due to this is unknown."

Educational Resources

- ➢ NOAA (National Oceanic Atmospheric Administration) Fisheries

An excellent resource for current population management and useful information on Steller sea lions.

https://alaskafisheries.noaa.gov/pr/steller-sea-lions

- ➢ The Marine Mammal Center, Hawaii

Information on rescuing and rehabilitating Stellers.

http://www.marinemammalcenter.org/education/
marine-mammal-information/pinnipeds/steller-sea-lion/

- ➢ Alaska Department of Fish and Game

Natural History and population updates. Good resource for population status.

- ➢ Kenai Fjords, National Park, Alaska

Educational materials and an interesting place to visit and see Stellers.

https://www.nps.gov/kefj/learn/nature/steller-
sea-lion.htm

- ➢ Washington Department of Fish and Wildlife

Conservation efforts.

http://wdfw.wa.gov/conservation/steller_sealions/

➤ World Wildlife Fund

Conservation efforts.

http://wdfw.wa.gov/conservation/steller_sealions/

➤ University of Washington

Center for Conservation Biology

http://conservationbiology.uw.edu/research-programs/ssl-trites/